WEEKLY WR READER®

EARLY LEARNING LIBRARY

Great Americans

Sacagawea

Boca Raton Public Library, Boca Raton, FL

Monica L. Rausch

Reading consultant: Susan Nations, M.Ed., author/literacy coach/
consultant in literacy development

Please visit our web site at: www.garethstevens.com
For a free color catalog describing Weekly Reader® Early Learning Library's list
of high-quality books, call 1-877-445-5824 (USA) or 1-800-387-3178 (Canada).
Weekly Reader® Early Learning Library's fax: (414) 336-0164.

Library of Congress Cataloging-in-Publication Data

Rausch, Monica.
    Sacagawea / by Monica L. Rausch.
       p. cm. — (Great Americans)
    Includes bibliographical references and index.
    ISBN-13: 978-0-8368-7685-7 (lib. bdg.)
    ISBN-13: 978-0-8368-7692-5 (softcover)
    1. Sacagawea—Juvenile literature. 2. Shoshoni women—Biography—
Juvenile literature. 3. Shoshoni Indians—Biography—Juvenile literature.
4. Lewis and Clark Expedition (1804-1806)—Juvenile literature I. Title.
    F592.7.S123R38   2007
    970.004'97—dc22
    [B]   2006032588

This edition first published in 2007 by
Weekly Reader® Early Learning Library
A Member of the WRC Media Family of Companies
330 West Olive Street, Suite 100
Milwaukee, WI 53212 USA

Managing editor: Valerie J. Weber
Art direction: Tammy West
Cover design and page layout: Charlie Dahl
Picture research: Sabrina Crewe
Production: Jessica Yanke and Robert Kraus

Picture credits: Cover, title page, pp. 11, 13, 15 Michael Haynes/www.mhaynesart.com; p. 5 © Stapleton
Collection/CORBIS; pp. 6, 8, 16, 21 © The Granger Collection, New York; p. 9 Charlie Dahl/© Weekly Reader
Early Learning Library; p. 10 © Nancy Carter/North Wind Picture Archives; p. 14 © Bettmann/CORBIS;
p. 17 National Park Service/ Fort Clatsop National Memorial; p. 19 © Connie Ricca/CORBIS;
p. 20 © North Wind Picture Archives

Printed in the United States of America

1 2 3 4 5 6 7 8 9 10 10 09 08 07 06

Table of Contents

Cover and title page: Sacagawea was only about sixteen years old when she traveled with Lewis and Clark. She was very brave!

Chapter 1

A Shoshone Teenager

Carrying her two-month-old baby, Sacagawea (sa-kuh-juh-WEE-uh) set out with Meriwether Lewis, William Clark, and a group of **explorers**. Their goal? To explore lands from the Mississippi River to the Pacific Ocean. She traveled on foot, by boat, and on horseback for hundreds of miles. Sometimes she had little food for her and her son to eat. Sacagawea helped the explorers speak with other Native Americans and found paths through the Rocky Mountains.

Sacagawea was a Native American and a member of the Shoshone people. The Shoshone lived in what is now Idaho and Montana. Sacagawea was born in about 1788. When she was about twelve years old, a group of Indians called the Hidatsa raided her village. They took her and other Shoshones **prisoner**.

This painting shows a group of Hidatsa Indians dancing. The Hidatsa still live in what is now North Dakota.

5

Like the man shown here, Charbonneau was a French Canadian fur trader. He trapped and killed animals, trading their fur for money or goods.

Sacagawea went to live with the Hidatsa near what is now Bismarck, North Dakota. While there, she met a man named Toussaint Charbonneau. In 1804, the Hidatsa sold Sacagawea to Charbonneau, and Charbonneau married her.

Chapter 2

Meeting Lewis and Clark

In 1803, President Thomas Jefferson wanted to buy land that was west of the Mississippi River. Most people living there were Native Americans, but France claimed this land.

Lewis was a captain in the army and Jefferson's secretary. Jefferson hoped Lewis could find an easy way to reach the Pacific Ocean.

Jefferson wanted to know more about this land, so he asked Meriwether Lewis to explore it. Lewis gathered a group of men and supplies. He asked his friend William Clark to help lead the group.

In March 1804, Jefferson bought the land from France. Just two months later, Lewis, Clark, and their men sailed up the Missouri River. Their journey had begun!

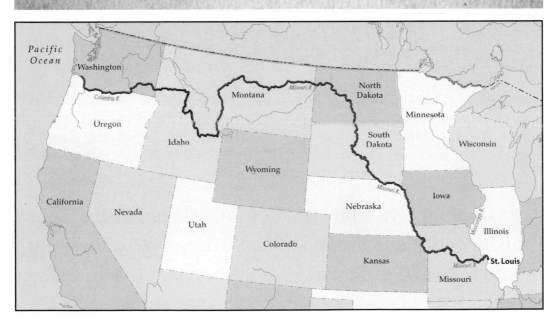

Lewis and Clark followed the Missouri River as it moved north and west. Their journey, shown in red, would take them to the Pacific Ocean and through many of today's western states.

Fort Mandan has been rebuilt to look the way the Lewis and Clark group first made it. There, the explorers talked to Native Americans to find out about the land they wanted to explore.

In October, the men reached the villages of the Hidatsa and the Mandan Indians. They built a fort near the villages and lived there for the winter. There, Lewis and Clark met Charbonneau and Sacagawea.

Lewis and Clark hired Charbonneau. They knew Sacagawea would come with him. Sacagawea would talk to the Shoshone people, and then she would tell Charbonneau what the Shoshone said. Charbonneau then would tell the Lewis and Clark party.

That winter, Sacagawea gave birth to a baby boy. Charbonneau named the child Jean Baptiste. Two months later, Sacagawea, Charbonneau, and their baby left the Hidatsa villages with the explorers.

Sacagawea and Charbonneau gave Lewis and Clark robes made out of the skin and fur of buffalo.

Chapter 3

To the Pacific Ocean and Back

The group sailed west on the Missouri River. In May 1805, the wind almost pushed over one of the boats. Water quickly flooded the boat, and papers and supplies began to drift away. Charbonneau did little to help. He was not used to boats. Sacagawea, however, calmly grabbed the floating papers and supplies. She saved a year's worth of work!

During July of 1805, Sacagawea started to see places she knew from her childhood. The explorers had reached the place where the Shoshone lived. She had not seen her homeland since she was taken prisoner by the Hidatsa. Soon, the group met some Shoshone people. When she saw them, Sacagawea danced with delight. The Shoshone chief was her brother, Cameahwait!

Sacagawea had not seen her brother for over four years. In this modern painting, she shows her son to Cameahwait.

Sacagawea helped Lewis and Clark speak with the Shoshone and buy horses from them. The men needed the animals to travel across the Rocky Mountains.

When they reached the mountains, the group could no longer travel by boat. They met with the Shoshone people to buy their horses.

Sacagawea and another Shoshone guided the group through the mountains. Sacagawea also found plants the men could use for medicine and for food, and she sewed and fixed their clothing.

Sacagawea was very kind. Once, the explorers had little food. She made some bread for Clark out of flour she was saving for her son.

After the travelers crossed the mountains, they met the Chinook Indians. Sacagawea spoke to them for the explorers. The Chinook gave them food and other supplies.

Sacagawea was also helpful when the group met other Native Americans. When other Indians saw her and her son with the men, they believed the explorers did not want to fight. They thought the men would not take a woman and child with them if they were planning a raid.

In November, the group finally neared the Pacific Ocean. Some of the men sailed down the Columbia River to the ocean. Lewis let Sacagawea go with them. She was so excited to see this huge body of water!

The men also wanted to build a fort for the winter. The group voted on a place to build it. Although women were not allowed to vote in the United States, the men counted Sacagawea's vote.

This copy of Fort Clatsop was built in 1955. It is close to where the explorers built their fort.

Chapter 4

Homeward Bound

In March 1806, the group left the winter fort. When they reached what is now Idaho, the group split up. Sacagawea helped Clark find a path through the mountains to the south. Lewis went through the mountains in the north. They all finally reached the Hidatsa villages in August. Sacagawea was home!

Lewis and Clark paid Charbonneau $500 for his help and the help of Sacagawea. Later, they gave him some land, too. Sacagawea received nothing for her hard work.

The men still needed to travel to St. Louis in what is now Missouri. They said good-bye to Sacagawea, Charbonneau, and Jean Baptiste. Clark liked Sacagawea's son and was especially sad to leave him.

This statue of Sacagawea carrying her son is in Bismarck, North Dakota, near Sacagawea's home.

In 1809, Sacagawea, Charbonneau, and their son visited Clark in St. Louis. Clark told them he could care for and teach their son. Two years later, Sacagawea and Charbonneau left the child with Clark and returned home.

In 1812, Sacagawea gave birth to a daughter. After her daughter was born, Sacagawea grew sick. She died in December 1812. She was only twenty-five years old.

Clark *(above)* had a special name for Sacagawea's son — "Pomp" or "Pompy." Clark liked to watch him dance and play.

Many statues have been made to honor Sacagawea. A mountain peak, a state park, a lake, and a river have all been named after her. In 2000, the U.S. government made a gold dollar coin to honor this kind, strong, and brave Native American woman.

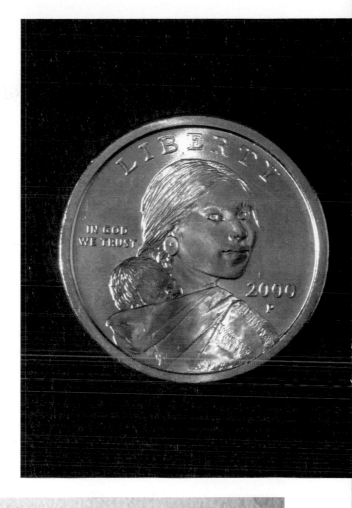

No one painted Sacagawea's picture when she was alive. Today, artists can only imagine what she looked like.

Glossary

claimed — said that something is owned

explore — travel over and learn about

explorers — people who travel looking for new information about places and things

hired — asked a person to do a job

homeland — the area where someone was born and grew up

prisoner — a person who is not free to move about and who is under the control of another person or people

raided — surprised and attacked

secretary — a person who keeps records in order and who writes letters for another person

supplies — items, such as food, clothing, or tools, needed to survive

For More Information

Books

Sacagawea. Raintree Biographies (series).
D. L. Birchfield (Raintree Publishers)

Sacagawea. Photo-illustrated Biographies (series).
Barbara Witteman (Bridgestone Books)

Sacagawea. Native American Biographies (series).
Rachel A. Koestler-Grack (Heinemann Library)

Sacajawea. All Aboard Reading (series). Joyce Milton
(Grosset and Dunlap)

Web Sites

Sacajawea: Indian Guide
www.enchantedlearning.com/explorers/page/s/sacajawea.shtml
Short biography on Sacagawea

The Weekly South Dakotan: South Dakota History
www.sd4history.com/index.htm
Entries for Unit 2 give information on the journey of Lewis, Clark,
and Sacagawea

Index

About the Author

Monica L. Rausch has a master's degree in creative writing from the University of Wisconsin-Milwaukee, where she is currently teaching composition, literature, and creative writing. She likes to write fiction, but sticking to the facts is fun, too. Monica lives in Milwaukee near her six nieces and nephews, to whom she loves to read books.